Preschc
Number Writing
(1 - 10)
for Left-Handed kids

This Book Belongs To

All rights reserved. No part of this book may be reproduced or used in any way or form or by any means whether electronic or mechanical, this means that you cannot record or photocopy any material ideas or tips that are provided in the book.

Book by Prachi Dewan Sachdeva and Sachin Sachdeva

About the Book

This is a perfect Preschool writing Workbook with coloring pages for special LEFT HANDED kids who want to learn numbers and improve their writing skills.

Languages that are written left-to-right, like English and all other common languages, are physically challenging to write for the left handers. And if a left-handed child is not taught how to write correctly, the child may develop messy form of writing that will stay with them even when they grow adult.

The Writing direction guides given in this book will help Parents and kids follow the right format of writing numbers and thereby enhance their writing. Full page of number writing practice for each letter will ensure kids have enough practice to master the same.

Highlights of the Book:
1. 10 pages of handwriting practice designed to make learning comfortable for left handed kids, with initial letters as trace and write.
2. 10 Coloring pages, one against each letter writing page ensures to keep the kids encouraged as they progress their learning of numbers.
3. Bonus 10 Activity Worksheets will not only retain kids' interest and motivate them but with Parent's rating these will ensure learning in the right direction.
Overall it is the perfect Tool for Home learning or Pre-schooling kids on Number Writing.

Prachi Dewan Sachdeva and Sachin Sachdeva are in the education field since 2002 and with a kid aged 9 have faced many challenges involved in parenthood, so now we have decided to help all the parents and teachers around with early learning of the kids and how to make it easy and fun.

By Prachi Dewan Sachdeva

Writing Guides

1 2 3 4
5 6 7 8
9 10

Let's Count 1 - 10

☆ 1

☆☆ 2

☆☆☆ 3

☆☆☆☆ 4

☆☆☆☆☆ 5

☆☆☆☆☆☆ 6

☆☆☆☆☆☆☆ 7

☆☆☆☆☆☆☆☆ 8

☆☆☆☆☆☆☆☆☆ 9

☆☆☆☆☆☆☆☆☆☆ 10

Let's Practice Writing 1

1

Let's Color
1 Cherry On 1 Cup Cake

1

1

Very Very Yummy

Let's Practice Writing 2

2

Let's Color
2 Beautiful Bags

Vacation Time

Let's Practice Writing 3

3

Let's Color
3 Gifts with bows

Full of Surprises

How Many?

How Many _____?

How Many _____?

How Many _____?

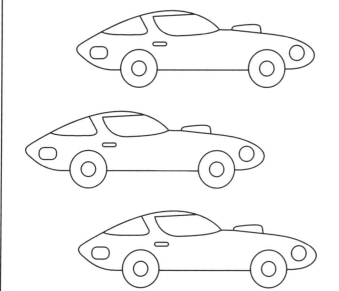

How Many _____?

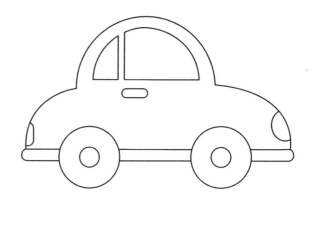

Parent's Rating

Count and Color

Parent's Rating

Let's Practice Writing 4

4

Let's Color
4 lovely Flowers

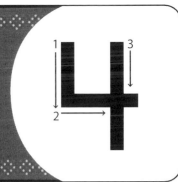

So Beautiful

Let's Practice Writing 5

5

Let's Color
5 Pretty Butterflies

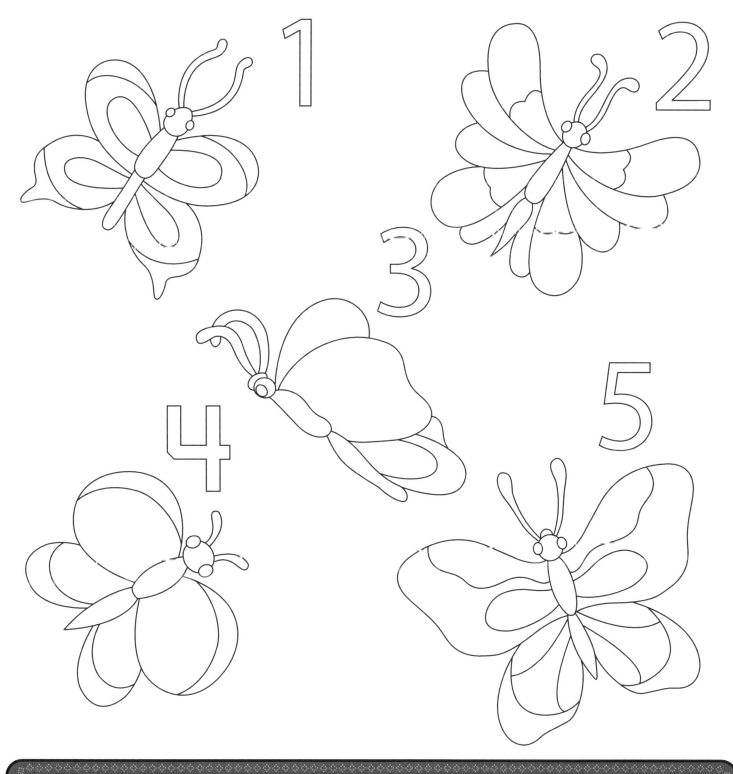

Lovely and Colorful

Count and Color

Parent's Rating ★★★★★

Count and Color Ship Helm

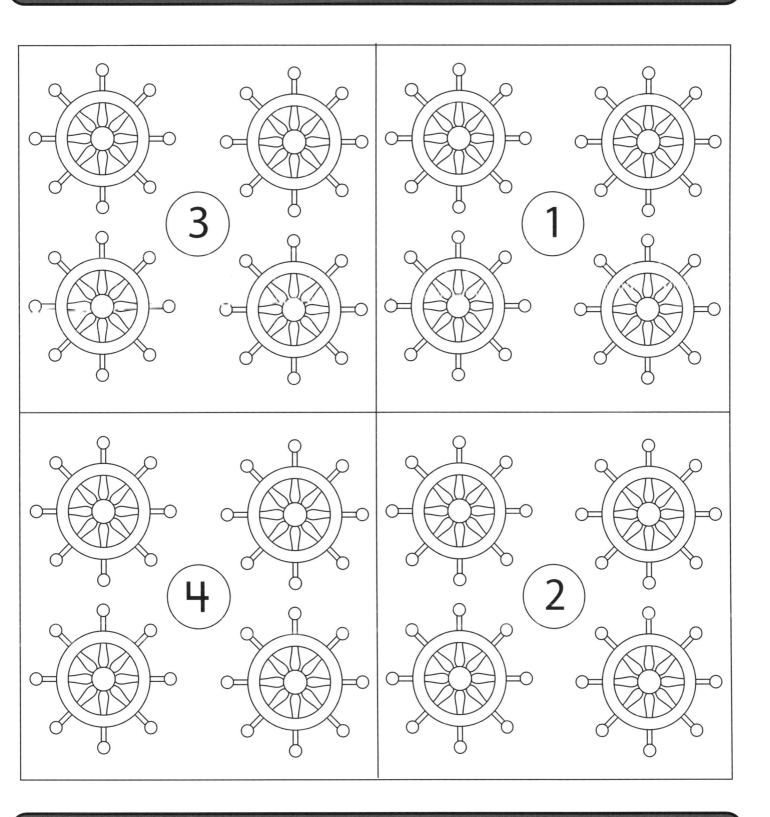

Parent's Rating

Let's Practice Writing 6

6

Let's Color
6 Gorgeous Fish

Swim Swim Little Fish

Let's Practice Writing 7

7

Let's Practice Writing 7

Let's Color
7 Fine Envelopes

Post from Friends and Relatives

Let's Practice Writing 8

8

Let's Color
8 Christmas Socks

8

Put Wishes for Santa

Color the Magical Numbers

1 - Yellow   2 - Blue   3 - Green   4 - Pink
5 - Purple   6 - Orange   7 - Red

Parent's Rating

Count and Color

Parent's Rating

Let's Practice Writing 9

9

Let's Color
9 Balls

Go and Play

Let's Practice Writing 10

10

Let's Color
10 Yummy Candies

Be Careful With Your Teeth

Count and Color the Picture

How many? Write the number.

Parent's Rating

Complete the Train

Parent's Rating

Build the Builder

Join the Numbers and Color the Image

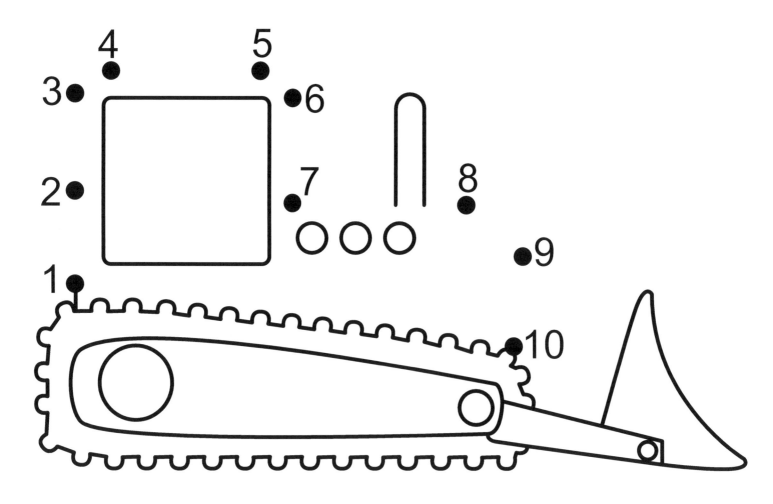

Parent's Rating

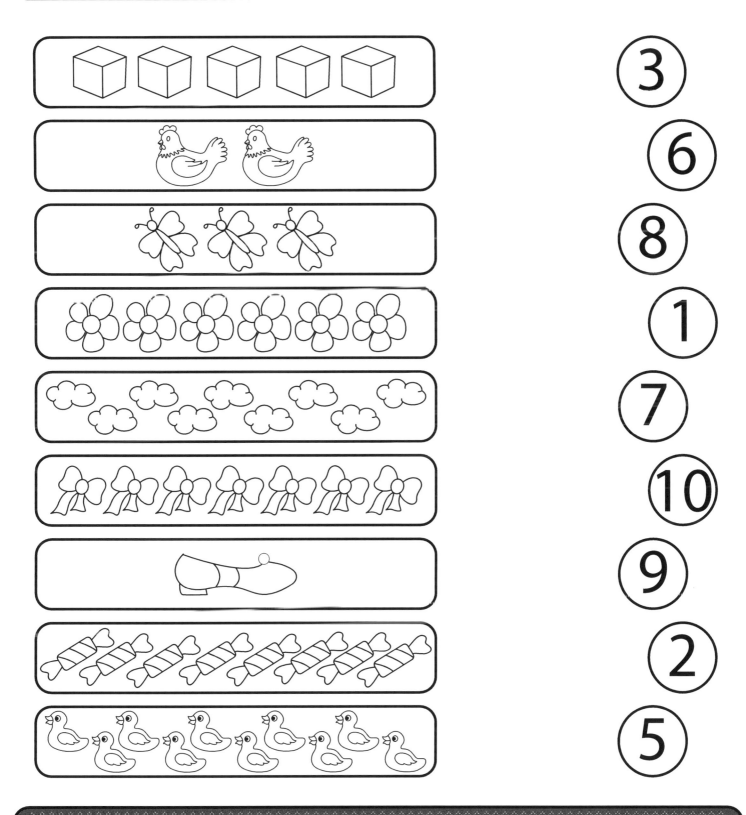

This is my first book for Left Handed children and I will be publishing more educational and learning content for children of all ages.

I will appreciate if you could leave your feedback on Amazon.

Best
Prachi Dewan Sachdeva

Manufactured by Amazon.ca
Bolton, ON